THE LOG OF THE "OLD UN"

THE LOG OF "THE OLD UN" FROM LIVERPOOL TO SAN FRANCISCO 1886

INTRODUCTION BY P. WYNNE-THOMAS

Published by J.W. McKenzie, 1994

This book was originally published in Exeter, for private circulation, in 1887.

It is here reprinted in exact facsimile, with the addition of a new Introduction by Peter Wynne-Thomas.

ISBN No. 0-947821-06-6

The story of cricket in North America during the second half of the nineteenth century is one of a war against baseball, a long drawn out conflict in which cricket progressively lost points and baseball won the hearts of America. By the time E.J. Sanders chose to go across the Atlantic, cricket had slipped into a minority sport and another fifty years saw it all but vanish.

Historians remember the great John Barton King who toured England with the 1908 Philadelphians and ended the summer at the head of the English first-class bowling averages. It is easy to believe that this was the pinnacle of American success on the cricket field. In a way it was, but underneath the handful of the top-class American cricketers was, by 1908, little more than a hidden chasm. When they retired the void was revealed. The general American public had long since ceased to interest themselves in the game and no fresh talent arose to replace King and his colleagues.

Before the American War of Independence cricket, as far as one can tell from the scattered reports, was the popular summer game on the North American continent, the population of the East Coast being then largely of British stock and it being natural that the games most common in Britain should be carried on across the Atlantic. The War dealt a blow to cricket, since the game was associated with Britain and the break between the two countries meant that things British were to an extent frowned upon.

By the 1850s cricket had revived. The first match between the United States and Canada had been played in 1844, the venue being the St. George's Club Ground in New York. About 5,000 spectators attended the first day's play. The success was such that the following season saw two matches arranged, one in each country. This was unusual however and by 1859 the total of such contests was only ten, some years being blank for a variety of reasons. The 1859 match, in Toronto, was regarded as a trial for matches that had been arranged against George Parr's England side in September. This tour by a team of English professionals marks a new era in cricket's history - the first time an England side had travelled overseas. Discussions concerning a possible tour had taken place over several years, before financial difficulties had been solved.

The cost of this expedition was £750, this sum included a guarantee of £50 for each player, as well as the general expenses. The two gentlemen who arranged the trip from the North American side were W.P. Pickering of Montreal and R. Waller of New York. According to Fred

Lillywhite's account of the tour, some 25,000 spectators turned out to watch the match in New York and such was the interest in the matches that arrangements were made for an additional game at the end - in late October with snow in the air. This last game naturally failed to attract the public. Lillywhite goes on to say "On Saturday October 22 no play took place owing to a heavy fall of snow, but a game of base-ball was got up among the players of that game and a portion of the English party, and which took place on the base-ball ground, about a mile from the cricket ground... Caffyn played exceedingly well, but the English thought catching the ball the first bound a very childish game."

Alexander Cartwright had formulated the basic rules of modern baseball in 1845 and in the first year as Parr's cricket tour, the first organisation connected to baseball was set up.

The Civil War commenced in 1861 - Lincoln's call for 75,000 volunteers was made on April 15 1861 just when arrangements were being made for the coming season. Very little cricket was played in the next four years, though baseball was played by the military, being an easier game to set up. This assisted the popularity of baseball, at a time when cricket could not compete. The international United States v Canada match was abandoned for the duration of the war and did not resume until 1865.

A second English side, like the first all-professional, crossed the Atlantic in 1868, playing five matches in the States and one in Canada. In addition the cricketers played several baseball matches.

The first all-amateur England team went out in 1872, organised by the then Secretary of M.C.C., R.A. Fitzgerald. The sponsors of the team just guaranteed to cover the players' expenses. Baseball was now thoroughly entrenched in American life. Fitzgerald wrote:

"Time is money here, and there is no denying that much of that valuable commodity is egregiously cut into ribbons at cricket. Americans might learn much, if they chose, from our noble game: if it inculcates one thing, it preaches and practises patience, it enforces self-control, it eliminates the irascible, it displays the excellence of discipline, it is more eloquent than Father Mathew on temperance and sobriety. With all respect for base-ball and its disciples, we believe that it principally encourages the two leading failings of American character - ultra-rapidity, quicksilver-sosity, or whatever else of lightning proclivity you like to call it, and ardent speculation."

There was a great improvement in the fixtures for this tour compared with its predecessors, in that the matches were played between August 22 and September 27, whereas it was mid-September before the first matches on the earlier visits. This meant that the weather was more agreeable and the matches well attended. Arthur Haygarth in his notes on the tour stated:

"For each match each gentleman cricketer received from their opponents 600 dollars in gold."

Haygarth had extracted this from a newspaper report, which like many such, was totally without foundation and he printed a correction deleting the comment in a later volume.

The fourth English tour reverted to an all-professional set up and was organised by J.P. Ford, a member of the Nottingham Town Council, who had business interests in America. More ambitious than previous tours it involved twelve matches, the previous programmes had been six, eight and six respectively.

It paid its way due to the great crowds who watched the match against fifteen of Philadelphia. For the first time on any visit to date one match against a local club was eleven a side. The local club was overwhelmed.

In the autumn of 1881, Lillywhite, Shaw and Shrewsbury decided to take a team to Australia and New Zealand, but to travel via America. The five matches in the States proved financially disastrous. In San Francisco less than one hundred spectators turned out. The local side knew little about the game and some of the crowd demanded their money back. It was the end of tours of professional cricketers to North America. Those who paid to watch were now devoted to baseball. The National League had been set up in 1876 and a rival league appeared in 1882.

So cricket was a 'gentleman's game' when, in 1885, E.J. Sanders decided to arrange a tour, playing eight matches, two in Canada and six in the States.

Edward James Sanders was a partner in the Exeter Bank and lived at Stoke House, Exeter. He was educated at Harrow and Cambridge, though not in the Eleven at either. However, he was a keen member of the Exeter Club and the leading light for Devonshire, struggling, as Hon. Secretary, to keep the County Club in existence. Ill-health meant that he could take no active part from 1897 and in November 1897 the County Club was dissolved. Ned Sanders died on October 27, 1904 having been more or less confined to his home for several years. He was aged fifty-two.

To captain his 1885 team, Sanders picked his former colleague in the Devon and Exeter sides, Parson Thornton. Thornton's brother, Albert, also joined the tourists. Both brothers were in 1885 associated with the Kent County side. However, the two Surrey cricketers in the party, W.E. Roller and C.E. Horner, took most of the honours, the former as a batsman and the latter as a bowler.

The first tour was a great success and the two major matches, against Philadelphia, saw attendances of eight or nine thousand. Each team won one match. Philadelphian cricket was dominated by the Newhall family and three brothers played in the Philadelphian side. Dan Newhall being the captain. His two not out innings of 43 and 37, the highest scores for his side, went a long way toward securing Philadelphia's win in the first game.

The 'New York Commercial Advertiser' seemed to believe that the battle between cricket and baseball was not yet decided:

"It is believed by some Americans that cricket will very soon supersede the game of baseball, especially as a gentleman's game. It is conducted in a quiet manner and without the usual howling that marks the game of baseball."

E.J. Sanders was encouraged by the hospitality he and his team had received in North America and by the crowds which attended the matches, he therefore determined to repeat the visit again in 1886 and commemorated the tour with a short account written by the "Old Un".

"Old Un" was the nom de plume of William Clulow Sim. He had been born in Madras in 1832, but was educated by Haileybury College. He joined the Indian Civil Service, but was compelled to retire early due to ill-health and he resided at Clyst St George, near Exeter. He was elected Honorary Secretary to the Devonshire County Club when the club was founded in 1861. In the late 1870s it was revealed that Sim had, in fact, been financing the County Club out of his own pocket for several years. He continued in office until 1889, when E.J. Sanders assumed the unenviable role. Little is known of his performances on the cricket field, but he was, as can be ascertained from the brief details given, a great lover of the game. In 1886 he volunteered to act as scorer for Sanders' Team to America and afterwards wrote his impressions of the tour, privately printing his 'Log'.

The tourists began their programme with a two day match against Staten Island. There had been two days for practice before the game and it was expected that the local club would prove a powerful combination, since the side included two professionals who had played first-class cricket for Nottinghamshire. Fred Butler, a newphew of the famous George Parr, was engaged by Staten Island in 1885 and 1886, but refused terms in 1887 and returned to England. He then reappeared for Nottingham. However, in 1900 he emigrated back to Staten Island, living there until he died in 1923. George Lane had first played for Staten Island in 1879; the best left arm bowler in America, he took 65 wickets and 4 runs for Staten Island in 1883. Later he set up a sports outfitters at Haverford College and died there in 1917. A third Staten Islander with strong English connections was Cyril Wilson, who had played as an amateur for Somerset.

Lane took five wickets and Butler three in the tourists' fair total of 203, but on the second day the Staten Island batting collapsed and Sanders' combination had an easy win.

After a few days of sightseeing, the tourists crossed into Canada. Canada did not possess the numbers of English professionals, who spent their summers south of the border, so it was a purely amateur side which represented Ontario, in Toronto. The English side won the game with ease and then travelled by boat through Lake Ontario and along the St Lawrence to Montreal. Despite fielding sixteen men, the local Montreal side was overwhelmed and Roller picked up twenty wickets in the match.

An overnight sleeper took the team to Boston, where another Nottingham professional, Chambers, was included in the American side. He captured ten wickets in the match at six runs apiece and Sanders' team won by the close margin of three wickets - there had been a similarly close game in the 1885 fixture, Sanders winning by 16 runs, with Chambers taking six wickets for 34 in the first innings. A second game in Boston began immediately the first had ended, but with only a day and a half allowed, it drifted to a draw.

Another overnight train journey took the side to Baltimore. The ground, about seven miles outside the city, was one of the best in the States, Baltimore fielded eighteen men, but were beaten by an innings.

The two great matches were against Philadelphia. To give some idea of the contrast between these games and the rest of the schedule, the largest attendance at any of the other matches was about 800. In Philadelphia 5,000 turned out on both the second and third days of the first match. In

1885 each team won one match; on this second visit the Englishmen won the first game by an innings and the second by six wickets. The Philadephians did not include any professionals. K.J. Key hit a brilliant hundred, with only one chance late in his innings in the first game and seemed to demoralise the American attack.

The only other game was on the Staten Island Ground against All New York. New York included Fred Butler and another Notts professional, Henry Tyers, who had just hit a century for the Players v Gentlemen. Both Notts men failed with the bat, though Tyers took five for 16 in Sanders' first innings which gave New York a lead of 68. The end of the match saw a marvellous dinner-dance. It went on to the small hours and meant that four of the team missed the last ferry back to New York. They hired a boat which let in water, and though their rowing was hampered by a drunken boatman, they completed the four mile journey in two hours. Mr Sanders, deep in water, directed matters from the stern.

A thoroughly enjoyable tour, which produced an improved record compared with the 1885 trip, ended with an exceedingly rough voyage back to Britain.

Of the twelve members of Sanders' side, three died before the end of the century. Cobb caught typhoid fever shortly after the team returned and died in Banbury in November of 1886. Cottrell, who was an outstanding member of Esher C.C., died in 1897 - he was a member of the Stock Exchange. Rev. A.T. Fortescue, vicar of Hinton in Lincolnshire died in 1899. E.H. Buckland, who never really achieved as much on the cricket field as had been expected, was a master at Winchester when he died in 1906 aged forty-one.

J.A. Turner's career in county cricket, for Leicestershire, ended when he lost the sight of an eye whilst playing rackets in 1893. He died in 1924. Welman kept wicket for Somerset occasionally until 1901. He died in 1931. The following year saw the death of Sir Kingsmill Key, 'a man of most original views, an always philosophic cricketer and an imperturbable captain.' He played for Surrey for twenty three years and led the county for six. H.W. Bainbridge led Warwickshire from 1888 to 1902 and then was appointed Hon. Secretary of that County Club, a post he held until his death in 1940. W.E. Roller, like Bainbridge, served his county, Surrey, behind the scenes when his playing days were at an end. He was regarded as the best Cambridge cricketer not to be awarded his blue. Ill-health ended his county career in 1990. Roller died in 1949. The longest surviving member of the team was T.R. Hine-Haycock, who died aged ninety-one in 1953. He was also the last survivor of the famous Oxford side which beat the Australians in 1884. He had been vicar of Christ Church, Greyfriars, which was bombed during the war and at his death was the senior priest-in-ordinary to the Queen.

The two matches by the tourists against Philadelphia are considered as 'first-class'. If cricket had been on the increase in the States at this time and American had been granted Test Match status prior to 1914, then it is not too far fetched to say that these games by Sanders' side would now be regarded as Test Matches - the two 1888/89 'England' v South African Tests were surely of a lower standard.

Peter Wynne-Thomas
Nottingham
August, 1994

THE Log OF THE "Old Un"

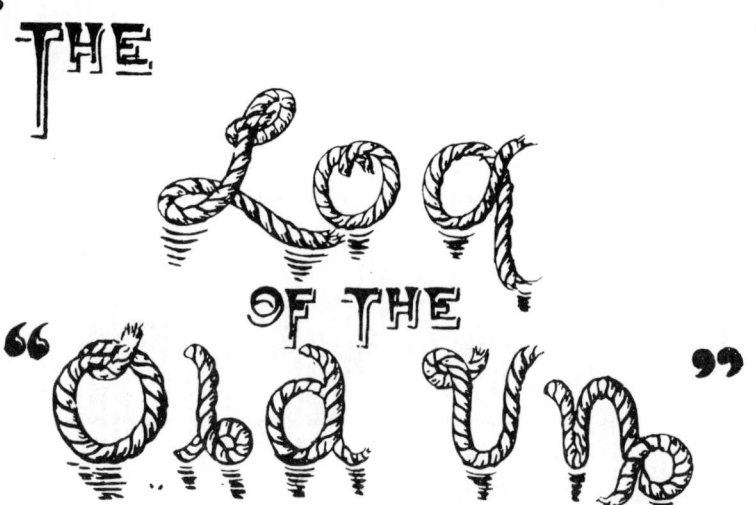

FROM LIVERPOOL TO SAN FRANCISCO

18 — 86

Printed for Private Circulation.

THE

LOG OF THE "OLD UN,"

FROM

LIVERPOOL TO SAN FRANCISCO.

Printed for Private Circulation.

DEDICATED,

WITHOUT PERMISSION,

TO THE

**MEMBERS OF THE ENGLISH CRICKETING
ELEVEN,**

WHO VISITED AMERICA AND CANADA IN 1886.

A PLAIN UNVARNISHED "LOG,"

A SIMPLE TRIBUTE OF REGARD THAT THE "OLD UN"

HOPES WILL BE ACCEPTED,

IN RECOLLECTION OF MANY PLEASANT DAYS ON

LAND AND SEA.

EXETER: H. S. ELAND, PRINTER.

THE LOG OF THE "OLD UN."

FROM LIVERPOOL TO SAN FRANCISCO.

1886.

Having long wished to pay my son in California a visit, I was easily persuaded by Ned Sanders, the Manager of the English Cricketing Eleven, to accompany his party across the Atlantic, in the unofficial capacity of Scorer, and, never once have I regretted the arrangement, for nicer or pleasanter companions, it would be difficult to meet on sea or land; but how could it be otherwise? for was not Roller in command with Arthur Fortescue as his Chaplain.

The team, itself, destined as it was to carry everything before it, was a really good representative one. The 'Varsities came to the front, with Fortescue (old blue), Bainbridge, Buckland, Cobb, Key and Turner, whilst 'the Gentlemen' were represented by Roller, Cottrell, Welman, Rotherham and R. T. Hine-Haycock, a "fine young English Cricketer, one of the present time"!! A good *all round* Eleven, of which, as far as physique was concerned, "Tristie" was the roundest of them all! to them, is this log, dedicated *without permission*. Their performances in the several matches that they played, will be found at the end, and they may well be congratulated on gaining an *unbeaten record*.

The "Key" of the team "wound" up well with "a century" in Philadelphia, clearly showing that though keyless watches in America are first rate things, a Keyless Eleven in the States would be a mistake. Roller and Turner might perhaps suggest that no watches at all would be better, theirs having been stolen in New York. These were the only things I believe that were stolen during the whole trip, for all attempts, frequent though they may have been, to steal the hearts of any of the Eleven, met with signal failure, and no wonder, for though American "belles" ring well, the "belles" of merry England ring out a still more melodious sound, at least to English ears—but enough of sentimentality, for what has the "Old Un," who is all "*years*" and yet "no *ears*," got to do with such subjects! as dear old Bob Grimston* would have said,

"It ain't Cricket,
"So shut up 'Old Un' and, parson-like, 'Stick to your text,'"

Well, Thursday, August 19th, saw us steaming out of Liverpool Docks on board the "Adriatic," White Star line, with Capt. Purcell as Commander, and about the nicest and most obliging man in the fleet, Mr. Russell, as Purser; but stop! are we all on board? No! *one wanting*, and the Manager's eyes are anxiously cast in the direction of a steam tug that was approaching with a few late passengers, amongst whom, with his ulster coat around him, was seen, gracefully seated on an empty bucket, the manly form of the absent one, who,

---

* The late Honble. Robert Grimston, well known as the keenest supporter of the game, and the most highly respected and esteemed man in the whole worl—"Sans peur et sans raproche."

utterly regardless of the Manager's anxiety, stepped on board humming to himself a classic ditty, the burden of which sounded like

" Tooral—ri—tooral—ri—teh."

Capt. Purcell is well known as one of the best Commanders in the Service, and no higher compliment could have been paid him than the remark of an American passenger who had made frequent passages: "When the captain's awake I guess we can all go to sleep," and the captain had to keep awake, for it was not long before a thick fog and mist set in, and kept all hands on the look out. Our fellow passengers consisted of the usual run of mortals. There was a fat lady who caused some conjecture, and a thin lady, whom everybody pitied. There were belles from Chicago, and emigrants from the Sister Isle; in fact, some 800 all told, of whom about 180 were saloon passengers; and last, but not least, was "Roguie," a friend of Welman's, and a perfect "*lion*" when roaring the chorus to a well-known Chelseaonic ballad ! ! !

August 20th, four a.m., saw us at Queenstown, and having taken in the mails, we started about one p.m., and very soon our trouble commenced. Most of the passengers succumbed at once, but the "team" held together till dinner time when the "*Rot*" began !! An Uppingham crack, finding it was all "*up in him*," retired in a hasty but still graceful manner, and others, in the course of time, followed his example. The honor of holding out altogether rested with the **occupants** of State Room No. 18. Fortescue, **Welman** and the "Old Un," to whom the ship owe nothing, they never having missed a meal from Liverpool to New York. Rotherham, too, held its own, and though Neptune " pitched 'em up a bit," managed to keep his victuals down ; and, like in his first match at New York, " carried his bat " after a freely-hit innings of four meals a day.

Sunday, 22nd, was commemorated by Service in the morning and by a heavy gale from the north-west in the afternoon, which made things pretty lively for passengers and crew. The second officer was washed into the lea-scuppers by a heavy sea that nearly took him overboard, and by which he was severely hurt. When the Cricketers recovered, and found their sea legs, they amused the passengers with " ship's cricket," in the course of which Tristie sent a favourite bat of Cottrell's into the sea, a tribute to Neptune that Roller remarked had probably never been paid before. As Cottrell refused to jump overboard to its rescue, and the Captain declined to lower a boat, that bat is, in all probability still " bobbing around " in mid ocean. Another game called " Come along round," afforded much entertainment, whilst whist, poker, whisky-cocktails, and other insinuating American drinks, taken in moderation with plenty of fun and frolic, helped to pass the time, till on Sunday the 29th, about 8.30 a.m. the passengers all filed down to confront the Custom House officers at New York. We had arrived and anchored off Sandy Hook the night before.

And now for a word as to " our manager." A complaint book had been bought, and everyone was requested to enter any real or imaginary grievance. but beyond the fact of his having neglected to provide a bottle of salad oil to pour on the troubled waters of the Atlantic, the pages remained blank. Bravo Ned! you deserve something more than a *cordial* vote of thanks, and I am sure the whole of the Eleven will gladly drink your health at your own expense as often as you like, and in any cordial you please!

New York certainly gave us a warm reception—too warm to be pleasant, and sadly demoralising to collars and cuffs. We all adjourned to the Brunswick Hotel, Fifth Avenue, where a good bath soon made us at peace with all mankind, for our tempers had been badly ruffled at the Custom House. Breakfast, with iced melons—quite an institution—having been disposed of, we separated in different directions, not at all sorry to be on dry land once more. Cyril Wilson and Eyre, who were part of a deputation from the Staten Island Cricket Club, carried off Welman, Fortescue, Cotterell, Rotherham and myself, whilst the rest of our party were also kindly looked after and hospitably entertained.

Monday the 30th was devoted to sight-seeing and practice. A single wicket match between the purser and myself resulted in an easy victory for the ship, and though my pride suffered not, from a nasty fall, my person did, and I limped about for some days a wiser but a *sorely* injured man! None the less, however, did I thoroughly enjoy a dinner given by the Eleven to my late opponent, and in which I was allowed to join. The feast was spread in the big public dining-room of the hotel, and passed off with great *eclat*. The speeches would have been most excellent, and the feeling way in which the purser returned thanks, would have been most touching, had "liberty of speech" been allowed; but the right royal way in which we drank his health was something tangible. "For he's a jolly good fellow" was on everyone's lips, but the certainty of being "chucked out" stopped any overt demonstration, though it did not prevent our drinking his health "again and again." Verily it was a pleasant dinner, and answered the purpose intended, which was to show our due appreciation of the purser's kindness and attention to all alike.

New York is a wonderful city. The inhabitants seem to know it too, and feel justly proud of their magnificent buildings, and their truly magnificent bays. The city is well mapped out, and, by the help of elevators and tramcars, easily traversed. These elevators, or railways above the streets, run in a level with the "second floor fronts" of the houses, whilst the tramcars run in a level with the kitchens; an observant traveller is thus enabled to form a pretty fair estimate of the domestic arrangements of the houses on each side of the street. For a fixed sum one can go either the whole or any portion of the distance that the cars run; ten cents go a long way in this manner, but a dollar goes nowhere in the shops. The public buildings, like everything else are on a gigantic scale, and necessitate the use of the lifts, but nothing strikes a stranger so much as the way the elevators twist round the corners of crooked streets.

The Stock Exchange is a lively sight, a spot where fortunes are made and lost, also on a gigantic scale. Old Dominie Sampson would certainly ejaculate "prodigious" could he see the activity displayed in the universal hunt for the mighty dollar, and the dollery look occasioned thereby. Even the children cut their wisdom teeth early in life. A Yankee "*child*" may be an expression, but is not a reality, for even the babies are born, grown up, and a New York Arab, combines the cuteness of a coon with the sharpness of a razor.

Tuesday and Wednesday were devoted to the first match between the Eleven and the Staten Island Club, and resulted in an easy victory for the Englishmen. As a straw will sometimes show the direction of the wind, so small matters may well indicate the "go ahead" peculiarities of our American Cousins. The ground on which the match was played was three months before a flourishing apple orchard, 193 apples were grubbed up, the grass had grown and the ground played fairly well. Three months!! Why it would take that time for us in the Old County to *think* about it, and three months more to enter into arrangements with a celebrated woodcutter to bring his axe, for he alone could do the job in the stipulated time, provided he had got "no (other) work to do."

On Tuesday night the Club entertained the visitors at dinner in the Club House, giving them a sumptuous repast and much drink. Speeches and songs followed and a lively evening was spent, but no impression was made on any of the visitors, some of whom found a training on Scotch whiskey, very useful on an emergency of this kind, and so to bed with a cool head.

Good luck to the Islanders, for they treated us with much kindness, and did their level best to make us feel at home.

On Wednesday night we went to the Casino Theatre,

where two boxes were kindly placed at our disposal, and after spending Thursday and Friday in New York sight seeing, we wished our many friends good bye and started early on Saturday, 4th September, for Niagara, by the York and Erie line, and a precious shaking we got! In this journey we were accompanied by Mr. Eyre, a real jolly good fellow, and a keen supporter of the noble game, to whom our Eleven owe much thanks. This line follows the course of the Delaware River, and passes through very fine river scenery but as it naturally curves a good deal, and as the engine drivers seldom think it necessary to slacken speed, the jolting was a "caution," the cars pitched and rolled like a ship at sea, and a sensation nearly akin to *mal de mer* was the result. Twenty-five miles an hour round a sharp curve would make a timid passenger on the Great Western at home open his eyes and "sit up." Here it was thought nothing of, and in a short time we also got, comparatively speaking, accustomed to it, but were not at all sorry to reach Niagara, by Buffaloe, about eleven p.m. Our train was late, so hungry but supperless, we had to retire to bed at the Cataract House. We felt bound, however, to see what we could of the river *in the dark*, and were no doubt much impressed thereby, but we should all have liked to have had some supper, and "glowered" at our manager, although we knew perfectly well that he didn't make the train late; still it was a relief to our hungry feelings. Ned, however, it was believed, had a biscuit or bit of one in his pocket, so walked off unconcernedly to bed. The Cataract House will always be connected in my mind with a loose waistcoat and a longing for breakfast,

Sunday, the 5th September, was partly spent in seeing the Falls, and well spent too, for a better sermon was heard in the roar of those Cataracts than could ever be preached in any church or by any clergyman. No one could have heard that roar without bringing home to himself the utter insignificance of man's strength, compared with the stupendous magnitude and greatness of the Creator, feeling, at the same time, the simple dependence and trust that all of us must place in God's great might, power, and love. Those of our party who had not been down to the Caves of the Wind now arrayed themselves in mackintoshes, and list slippers and went under the falls and through the spray, and so great was the concussion of the air with the vast volume of water, that the breath was quite taken out of our bodies. and it was as much as we could do to hold on to the single handrail that had been set up as a kind of protection to prevent being blown away. The great mass of water passed close over our heads in one mighty wave enveloping us in spray and almost taking away our senses. A lovely rainbow, seemed to start from and end at our very feet. To describe the grandeur of the Fall is impossible; the deafening roar, the swift current, the terrific dash, with the comparative smoothness of the pool below, within a few hundred feet of the Fall, must be seen to be realized, and the ablest artist in the world must fall far short of reality in attempting to depict one of Nature's grandest scenes. We then went to the whirlpool rapids, where Captain Webb was drowned, and could not but help reflecting how easily useful lives are thrown away in attempting to perform useless and hazardous achievements. The Cataract

House is very nice, clean and cheap. Knick-knacks of all kinds can be purchased at the Indian stores just opposite the hotel. Much were these stores patronized by the members of the Eleven, and great was the weeping and wailing when the omnibus carted off the Eleven and their purchases.

The Suspension Bridge, about two miles off and close to the whirlpool rapids, is the boundary between Canada and America, and here our luggage was overhauled by the Custom House Officers. We had left Niagara that afternoon the 6th September, about three p.m., and reached Toronto about 7.30 p.m. the same evening, putting up at the Queen's hotel.

Toronto beautifully situated on lake Ontario, is a fine Canadian city, and the centre of much trade in the *dry* goods line. It has a large and increasing population and many fine buildings.

The difference between the Canadian and American coinage is an everlasting trouble to those crossing the border.

On Tuesday, 7th September, the English commenced their second match, and on this occasion defeated the Ontario Association Club by eight wickets. Cricket is more likely to take root and prosper in Canadian than in American soil. It is not *fast* enough for the go-ahead Yankee, who much prefers his own national game of base ball—a game much resembling the rounders of our boyish days, except that instead of " *corking* " the runner, the ball is thrown to the base keepers—a decided improvement, as the ball is nearly as large and almost as hard as a cricket ball, so that a " corker " in the small of one's back, when thrown with "malice intent," would be a present pain and a sensation to be remembered for ever! A base ball match seldom lasts more than two or three hours, and is keenly watched by a crowd of *interested* spectators, who *make it hot* for the umpire should his decision be open to doubt, and adverse to the losing and largest faction. If one meets a man in the street with his arm in a sling, one broken leg, and an eye out, it may safely be conjectured that this "wreck of humanity" had been "adjudicating" at some recent *big* base ball match, and had to run the gauntlet of some two or three thousand infuriated lookers-on. The betting on the result of these matches runs high, and in the "Seven Dials" of the far West an umpire seldom gives a decision, unless he has a safe "bolt hole" in view and close by.

"It doesn't do, to put the dander up,
Nor with the feelings trifle
Of angry crowds, who often bear
A bowie knife and rifle."

On Tuesday evening, 7th September the whole Eleven and myself dined with Mr. Thomas, the Bursar of Marlborough College, and spent a pleasant evening.

On Wednesday, the 8th, the match was continued with the result already mentioned. Having a bit of a " toe " and a reminder of gout, I remained in the hotel, simply seeing some of the places pretty handy, and taking my "through ticket" for San Francisco, about ninety dollars worth! The American arrangement for railway travelling are far superior to ours in many ways. All the lines run in connection with each other, and one can book right through to any place at any of the different railway depôts, and on payment of a additional small sum break the journey *en route*. One's luggage is checked at the starting point, a numbered check fastened on to each package, and a corresponding check given to the passenger. At the end of the journey, or if one intends stopping at any place on the road, a railway official asks for the checks, and passes the luggage to a transfer car, asking where one wishes it sent, and on the payment of a small fee for each package the luggage is safely delivered. If one stops at any intermediate station, but does not want one's luggage, it goes on to the depôt to which it was originally checked and remains there till called for. Nothing can be simpler nor more convenient. One should never take a gun case loose, no railway company will check it, and it remains on one's hands, the case itself a burden, its contents anything but a "small bore." The best plan is to purchase a big American trunk and put as much as one can inside. The fewer packages one has the better, and a trunk, although almost as big as a wooden hut at Aldershot, gives no more trouble *to the owner* than a small hand portmanteau. A formidable thing to look at is one of these trunks, certainly not built for the top of a hansom cab, all big, some bigger, and the biggest about half the size of a Pickford's van! Still, they are well adapted for travelling in America.

On Wednesday evening I wished the cricketers goodbye and good speed after having spent several very pleasant days in their company, and it is impossible for me adequately to acknowlege the kindness they one and all showed the "Old Un," nor the considerate way in which they overlooked his many infirmities, and I must say a more cheery or nicer lot " together joined in the manly toil of cricket" it would be impossible to meet with anywhere

On Wednesday night, 8th September, at 11.35 p.m., I started on my long solitary journey to the " Far West," arriving at Chicago 6.30 p.m. on Thursday, the 9th September, in pouring torrents of rain with vivid flashes of lightning, and at the Palmer House I had my first introduction to a real American hotel, conducted on a public and private system. The entrance hall was crowded, a big fair being in full swing, and some Irish delegates in full force. I secured my key and found my way to a lift, and thence to a most comfortable suite of apartments, for the Palmer House is justly considered the best hotel in Chicago.

The railroad from Toronto to Chicago passes through a flat and well cultivated country, and running as it does at night, has sleeping cars attached to the ordinary carriages. During the night we crossed over (by Fort Edmund) the boundary between Canada and America, but as the luggage had been examined and passed at Toronto, the passengers were not disturbed. Chicago itself is intersected by a river, and so formed into blocks and celebrated for its huge pork-boiling establishments. Thousands of pigs are daily converted into sausages and other porkine delicacies, but the smoke that hangs about the city from the huge chimneys is *sometimes* very dense, for though the inhabitants consume some of their own pork, the chimneys do not consume their own smoke; the streets are broad and well paved. I was " up and about" pretty early, but failed to discover the famous machine that is said to convert live pigs into sausages, and sausages into live pigs. Perhaps I didn't get up early enough.

On Friday the 10th September, at 11.50 a.m., I started by the train from the Burlington Route Depôt for Council Buffs. The country is still very flat and made the most of, some portions resembling English parks, well timbered with oaks and chestnuts, and the grass quite green after the recent rains. Clover fields here and there looked as if they could hold a covey or two of partridges, but the only Yankee sportsman I saw was going about in his shirt sleeves, gun in hand, but nothing in bag, or rather trowser pockets. He told me birds were scarce, and a more villainous compound of loafer and poacher I never sat eyes on before. May I never see his like again !

About 6 p.m. we crossed the great Mississippi River from the Illinois State to that of Ohio. Burlington, a place of some importance, is on the west bank, and here was a big "lumber yard." Stacks and stacks of timber, cut up into all shapes and sizes, towering one above the other. The wood is floated down the river, conveyed to the saw mills and there cut up.

Saturday the 11th September, about 9.30 a.m., saw us at the end of our journey, or rather as far as Council Buffs, where, at the expenditure of thirteen dollars I had my luggage re-checked to San Francisco There is an hotel at the station, and "Omaha" is on the opposite side of the Missourie river, a magnificent stream, almost if not quite as broad as the Mississippi. The town of Council Buffs is about two miles from the station. We now enter the Union Pacific Railway Company's territory, for they not only own the line itself but considerable land as well. We were detained about an hour, in consequence of a collision that had occured seventy-five miles west of Omaha, and the travellers from San Francisco were twelve hours behind time in consequence. It seemed that their train had collided with a freight van, but, as in the old country, the railway officials were very reticent of information, beyond the fact that two people were killed and several injured, nothing further was heard of such a small matter! The same evening, about nine p.m., we left Omaha, and amongst my fellow passengers were some exceedingly nice Californians who were most civil, and took me, metaphorically speaking, by the hand; they pointed out all the chief objects of interest, and were most kind and obliging. The greater part of the journey was through prairie plains all along the La Platte river. These prairies extend for some hundreds of miles all round, and look arid, desolate and utterly uninteresting. At Cheyenne, where we stopped to feed at 6 p.m. on Sunday, 12th September, I swallowed my first American fly, and most likely many others, for they simply swarmed. From Cheyenne we gradually ascended till we reached Liarmie, the summit of a spur of the Rocky Mountains, about 8,700 feet above the level of the sea! The following morning, September 13th, we were still going through undulating prairie land, with nothing in sight all the day except a few deer in the distance, and the comical little prairie dogs, till we entered the Mormon State of Utah, when the whole nature of the country completely changed. We now found ourselves amongst hills of apparently lime-stone formation of great height. A river ran through a narrow gorge with a curious rock called "The Devil's Slide" and close by it a large fir tree bearing an inscription, "1,000 miles from Omaha." The valley here was cultivated like a garden, and being well irrigated was green and pleasant to the eye. Whatever the Mormons' idea of plurality may be, they showed a singularly keen notion of picking out a fruitful land with natural fortifications of great strength, the only access to the State from the East being through this narrow gorge. The scenery reminded me strongly of the hills of bonnie Scotland, and at one particular place I almost imagined myself, gun in hand, amongst the grouse on Dee side Aberdeenshire, though one missed the purple heathery hue so characteristic of our Northern braes.

At 6 p.m. we reached the township of Ogden, and here I had intended staying for a day, as it is the starting place for the Salt Lake country, but feeling no fatigue, and having no particular interest in the domestic arrangements of Brigham Young's successors, I had my traps transferred to another train, and started for San Francisco at 7 p.m. the same evening.

On the west of Ogden one passes through large alkaline plains, which even Mormon industry cannot reclaim. Nothing will grow on this sterile soil. The night was hot and sultry; the curtained sleeper felt like an oven, and a sleepless and uncomfortable night the result, but the morning was beautifully fresh and clear. On Monday the 14th, we were still puffing and panting through similar scenery, though we skirted the Taho river, which eventually enters and is lost in a large lake, and wound round several hills till about 10 p.m., when we crossed the Sierra Nevada mountains, and here the scenery became grand in the extreme. We were now in California, the boundary between the states of California and Utah, being at Reno, a place that we had passed two hours before, and where one ought to have stopped and taken a day train, but the moon was full and the night bright and clear, so I am not at all sure that moonlight, on this occasion, wasn't better than daylight. We passed over deep ravines, looking down on the snow-clad fir trees hundreds of feet below. The moon lit up the view, and the rocks and trees glistened in her light. We passed through miles and miles of snow sheds, but the peeps we got of the ravines below were simply lovely. I remained on the platform between the carriages till smoke and cinders drove me half-blind to my bunk. The Sierra Nevada range is one of the features of the country, and of itself well worth a journey of some thousand miles to see.

On the morning of the 18th September we breakfasted at Sacramento, and the monotony of our railway journey was now broken, for we crossed what I think was the estuary of the Sacramento river in a ferry-boat, said to be the largest ferry-boat in the world. It took over the whole train in one trip! We finally embarked in a steamer, crossed the end of one of the bays, of which San Francisco boasts three. A tram-car conveyed those who wished to go to the Palace Hotel, San Francisco, and thus my long railway journey from the Atlantic to the Pacific was ended. The American continent is a big one to cross, and on my return trip it was done in one continuous stretch of six days and six nights without my experiencing any great discomfort or fatigue. The Palace Hotel is the biggest in America, and perhaps in the world. It is built in the shape of a square, with a huge court-yard in the centre. The rooms rise tier above tier, with broad corridors all round each floor. The arrangements are perfect, and the charges moderate.

San Francisco is an enormous and still growing city, built apparently on no particular plan, but comprising every kind of architecture, and containing a most mixed and varied population. It is founded, not on a rock, nor on the sand, but on a portion of one of its bays, and is altogether one of the most extraordinary cities in existence. Some years ago it was, comparatively speaking, *nothing*; what it will be, who can tell?

And now my Log, long since changed from a *sea* to a *land* one, comes to an end, but as even a Log ought to be turned to some account before it is put on the fire, so this plain unvarnished one may perhaps be allowed to end with a few facts that may possibly be of some small kind of use, in some small kind of way to emigrants thinking of settling in California. I write with great diffidence, for a visit of but one month's short duration is not sufficient to enable anyone to do more than simply narrate what he has seen and heard, leaving others to draw their own deductions therefrom.

California is admitted to be the most fertile State in America. She is the garden of the West. Fruit of all kinds grow in the greatest abundance. Corn and wine are becoming the almost natural produce of this fruitful land. The climate, though hot in summer, is far healthier than in other less favoured States. Land, except in the vicinity of large towns, is comparatively cheap, but rapidly rising in value. Water, for irrigation purposes, is supplied very much on the Indian plan by large irrigation channels from the big rivers. These channels again supply smaller ones, and thus water can be carried all over the country; BUT there is ONE thing that the intending settler must constantly bear in mind and act up to. *He must work.* Manual labour in America is not considered derogatory; quite the reverse, and every young man settling there must off with his coat and "buckle to." Hired labour is so expensive that one must do all one can *oneself*, and the more one can do the better will one thrive. The question, "What to do with one's boys" is in the old country a difficult nut to crack. Here is an opening and a good one too. The usual plan adopted is for a young man to pay a premium, work, and gain experience for one year at some ranche, and if he has used his time to good purpose at the end of that period, he ought to be fit to manage a small ranche for himself, but it will be of no use unless he is *willing* to work, and to work hard.

It is the firm belief of many with whom I have conversed that in a few years California will have made such rapid strides that it will become one of the most important States in America. Railways are opening it out in all directions.

San Francisco, with its command of the Japan and China trade, which *now* **passes** through to New York, will, with increased steam communication, hold its own with its great rival in the East, and no doubt eventually, retain a large portion of the commerce that now passes through its golden gates. As I said before, I write with much diffidence, but I cannot help expressing my idea that there is a most brilliant future in store for the great great city of the far far West ; and as the prosperity of the city increases, so will that of the country around.

The " Lucern " valley, as I believe it is to be re-christened, lying to the South of San Francisco ; with the Sierra Nevada range of mountains on one side, and the coast range on the other is considered the most fertile portion of even this fertile State. A railway already runs through its whole length ; with San Francisco city as a terminus at one end and New York itself at the other, and it is thus in communication with all the chief cities in America. With these advantages already gained, one may easily prognosticate the position it will hold in the future greatness of the whole State. Land is to be had on fairly reasonable terms and in all directions.

I ask no one to emigrate, but merely mention the inducements that seem to me to be advantageous. Of other States I know nothing ; many of them may possibly possess even still greater advantages. I merely write of what I have seen. and now my log is ready to be put on the " dogs " of the fire-place, and I trust it will cast a cheerful blaze on all around. If it will but burn brightly and not splutter, the " Old Un " will be satisfied, for it will then be of some little use, and perhaps help to " keep a kettle boiling," without getting into " hot water " itself.

THE LOG OF THE "OLD UN." 23

FIRST MATCH AT NEW YORK.—English Team *v.* Staten Island C.C.
1st, 2nd, and 3rd September, 1886.

ENGLISH TEAM.

1st Innings.

H. W. Bainbridge, c Wilson, b McGregor	29
T. R. Hine-Haycock, b Lane	8
K. J. Key, b Henry	42
J. A. Turner, b Lane	13
Rev. A. T. Fortescue, c Smith, b Lane	6
E. H. Buckland, c Warburton, b Lane	0
A. R. Cobb, b Butter	47
W. E. Roller, b Butter	8
C. E. Cottrell, b Butter	8
H. Rotherham, not out	25
E. J. Sanders, b Lane	10
F. T. Welman, b Henry	0
Extras	7
	203

STATEN ISLAND C.C.

1st Innings.		2nd Innings.	
C. J. Wilson, b Cottrell	10	b Rotherham	6
J. R. Moore, c and b Roller	0	b Rotherham	6
Butter, c Welman, b Roller	0	c Turner, b Rotherham	28
W. M. Massey, run out	22	b Buckland	11
E. W. Kessler, b Rotherham	16	c Fortescue, b Hine-Haycock	10
E. McGregor, c Buckland, b Cottrell	8	b Rotherham	6
J. Henry, l b w, b Cottrell	6	c Buckland, b Turner	0
Lane, c and b Cottrell	1	b Rotherham	5
E. H. Outerbridge, c and b Cottrell	0	c and b Hine-Haycock	0
P. W. Smith, not out	3	c Roller, b Rotherham	0
A. C. Townsend, b Cottrell	0	b Rotherham	2
B. Warburton, b Cottrell	0	not out	0
Extras	8	Extras	7
	74		81

English Team won by an innings and 49 runs.

SECOND MATCH AT TORONTO.—English Team v. Ontario Cricket Association, 7th, 8th, and 9th September.

ENGLISH TEAM.

1st Innings.		2nd Innings.	
H. W. Bainbridge, b Gillespie	2	b Gillespie	0
T. R. Hine-Haycock, b Ferrie	0	not out	7
K. J. Key, c Hamilton b Gillespie	1	c Simpson, b Ferrie	4
J. A. Turner, c Hamilton, b Gillespie	11		
W. E. Roller, c Ferrie, b Gillespie	5	not out	2
A. R. Cobb, b Simpson	15		
E. H. Buckland, c Vickers, b Simpson	54		
Rev. A. T. Fortescue, not out	58		
C. E. Cottrell, c Guthrie, b Harley	8		
H. Rotherham, c Guthrie, b Ferrie	4		
F. T. Welman, b Wilson	3		
Extras	8	Extras	2
	169		15

ONTARIO C.A.

1st Innings.		2nd Innings.	
F. G. Allan, b Rotherham	0	b Roller	5
W. W. Vickers, b Cottrell	0	c Bainbridge, b Rotherham	0
H. Guthrie, c Key, b Cottrell	0	b Rotherham	0
A. H. Gillespie, c and b Cottrell	2	b Roller	11
F. Harley, c Roller, b Buckland	40	b Roller	1
A. C. Allan, b Cottrell	0	c Welman, b Hine-Haycock	45
W. W. Jones, b Rotherham	1	b Hine-Haycock	1
M. Hamilton, c Cobb, b Cottrell	13	c Rotherham, b Roller	2
R. B. Ferrie, c Turner, b Cottrell	7	st Welman, b Hine-Haycock	38
G. B. Simpson, b Buckland	0	c Bainbridge, b Cottrell	4
W. R. Wilson, not out	3	not out	0
Extras	6	Extras	4
	72		111

English Team won by eight wickets.

THE LOG OF THE "OLD UN." 25

THIRD MATCH AT MONTREAL.—Twelve of English Team *v.* Sixteen of Montreal, C.C., September 11th, 13th and 14th.

ENGLISH TEAM.
1st Innings.

H. W. Bainbridge, c Gough, b Sills	47
Rev. A. T. Fortescue, c Sillas. b Lacey	16
K. J. Key, b Savage	52
T. R. Hine-Haycock, c Boatus, b Gough	4
J. A. Turner, b B. T. A. Bell	57
E. H. Buckland, b Savage	25
A. R. Cobb, b Savage	14
W. E. Roller, not out	0
C. E. Cottrell, c and b Savage	2
H. Rotherham, c and b Stancliffe	20
E J. Sanders, not out	9
F. T. Welman, c Lacey, b Gough	0
Extras	11
	257

Sixteen of Montreal C.C. made—First innings, 85 ; second innings, 55. English Team won by an innings and 117 runs.

FOURTH MATCH AT BOSTON.—English Team *v.* Fifteen of Longwood C.C., September 15th, 16th, and 17th.

ENGLISH TEAM.

1st Innings.		2nd Innings.	
W. E. Roller, b G. Wright	28	c Stuart, b Chambers	4
H. W. Bainbridge, b G. Wright	3	c Hubbard, b Chambers	23
K. J. Key, c Hubbard, b G. Wright	0	b G. Wright	1
T. R. Hine-Haycock, b Chambers	0	b Chambers	4
J. A. Turner, c Curtis b Chambers	1	b Lovett	12
Rev. A. T. Fortescue, b Chambers	12	b Chambers	4
E. H. Buckland, c Chambers, b G. Wright	17	c Dutton, b Chambers	1
A. R. Cobb, c Haughton, b G. Wrigght	1	not out	9
H. Rotherham, c Chambers	5		
C. E. Cottrell, not out	9	not out	4
F. T. Welman, c F. Mansfield, b Chambers	1		
Extras	0	Extras	2
	77		64

Fifteen of Longwood C.C. made—First innings, 96 ; second innings, 43. English Team won by three wickets.

Fifth Match at Boston.—English Team v. Fifteen of New England, 17th and 18th September.

ENGLISH TEAM.

1st Innings.		2nd Innings.	
J. R. Hine-Haycock, c O'Hair, b Comber	0	b Pettitt	11
R. J. Key, b Hubbard	29	c G. Wright, b Comber	6
H. W. Bainbridge, b Pettit	14	c J. Mansfield, b Hubbard	16
Rev. A. T. Fortescue, c L. Mansfield, b Hubbard	5	b Pettitt	0
J. A. Turner, b Dutton	4	not out	11
E. H. Buckland, b Dutton	8		
A. R. Cobb, b Dutton	14	b Pettitt	25
C. E. Cottrell, not out	29	c Comber, b Wright	49
E. J. Sanders, b Dutton	1		
F. T. Welman, b Dutton	0		
Handford, c Brown, b Comber	1	l b w, b O'Hair	3
Extras	11	Extras	14
	116		135

Fifteen of New England C.C. made—First innings, 109. **Match drawn**

Sixth Match at Baltimore.—English Team v. Eighteen of Baltimore C.C., 20th, 21st, and 22nd September.

ENGLISH TEAM.

1st Innings.

H. W. Bainbridge, c Inglehart, b Brune	49
T. R. Hine-Haycock, b J. N. Steele	15
K. J. Key, run out	96
J. A. Turner, b Brune	13
E. H. Buckland, b Brune	6
A. R. Cobb, b Smith	3
Rev. A. J. Fortescue, c Marston, b Oldham	25
C. E. Cottrell, c Ridgley, b J. N. Steele	20
H. Rotherham, c S. T. Steele, b J. N. Steele	25
F. T. Welman, c W. Whitelock, b Brune	2
E. J. Sanders, not out	0
Extras	9
	263

The Eighteen of Baltimore made—First innings, 82; second innings, 117.

English Team won by an innings and 58 runs.

THE LOG OF THE "OLD UN."

Seventh Match at Philadelphia.—English Team *v.* All Philadelphia, 24th, 25th, and 26th September.

ALL PHILADELPHIA.

1st Innings.		2nd Innihgs.	
J. A. Scott, c Welman, b Buckland	18	c and b Buckland	31
G. S. Patterson, b Buckland	32	run out	19
W C. Morgan, junr., b Buckland	27	c Welman, b Buckland	3
R. S. Newall, c Welman, b Buckland	11	c sub, b Roller	25
W. Brockie, junr., c and b Buckland	0	b Buckland	1
E. W. Clarke, junr., b Turner	9	b Buckland	0
C. A. Newhall, b Turner	18	b Hine-Haycock	15
W. Scott, b Rotherham	6	c Roller, b Buckland	5
F. W. Ralston, junr., b Buckland	7	c Cottrell, b Roller	32
F. E. Brewster, not out	15	not out	1
H. J. Brown, b Cottrell	9	c sub, b Buckland	0
Extras	16	Extras	7
	168		139

ENGLISH TEAM.

1st Innings.

H. W. Bainbridge, c Brewster, b W. Scott	10
J. A. Turner, b C. A. Newhall	11
K. J. Key, c W. Scott, b H. J. Brown	109
W. E. Roller, c Clark, b H. J. Brown	75
T. R. Hine-Haycock, b H. J. Brown	5
E. H. Buckland, c Brewster, b C. A. Newhall	19
A. R. Cobb, c R. Newhall, b H. J. Brown	14
Rev. A. T. Fortescue, c C. A. Newhall, b H. J. Brown	31
C. E. Cottrell, c Morgan, b C. A. Newhall	2
H. Rotherham, c Morgan, b C. A. Newhall	27
F. T. Welman, not out	7
Extras	13
	323

English Team won by an innings and 16 runs.

EIGHTH MATCH AT NEW YORK, 27th and 28th September.—English Team *v.* All New York.

ALL NEW YORK.

1st Innings.		2nd Innings.	
W. R. Williams, c Rotherham, b Roller	14	c Buckland, b Roller	2
J. Y. Davis, c Hine-Haycock, b Roller	34	b Rotherham	0
Butler, b Roller	5	b Cottrell	5
Tyers, c Welman, b Roller	5	b Cottrell	0
A. Priestly, l b w Rotherham	16	c Cobb, b Cottrell	0
C. J. Wilson, c Cobb, b Roller	3	c and b Cottrell	17
J. H. Lambkin, b Cottrell	26	not out	10
E. Kessler, b Rotherham	2	b Cottrell	0
J. Cuddihy, b Cottrell	5	c Welman, b Cottrell	2
R. McGregor, not out	14	b Cottrell	0
J. L. Pool, b Cottrell	5	c and b Cottrell	0
Extras	14	Extras	5
	143		41

ENGLISH TEAM.

1st innings.		2nd innings.	
E. H. Buckland, run out	11		
T. R. Hine-Haycock, c Williams, b Tyers	1		
K. J. Key, c Kessler, b Tyers	14	not out	4
W. E. Roller, c and b Pool	8	not out	55
A. R. Cobb, b Lambkin	16		
Rev. A. T. Fortescue, b Lambkin	5		
H. W. Bainbridge, b Lambkin	9	c Pool, b Tyers	46
J. A. Turner, b Tyers	1		
H. Rotherham, b Tyers	8		
C. E. Cottrell, not out	5		
F. T. Welman, b Lambkin	0		
Extras	5	Extras	8
	83		113

English Team won by nine wickets.

THE LOG OF THE "OLD UN."

NINTH MATCH AT PHILADELPHIA. 1st, 2nd, and 4th October.—English Team *v.* All Philadelphia.

ALL PHILADELPHIA.

1st Innings.		2nd Innings.	
J. A. Scott, c Buckland, b Cottrell	9	b Buckland	25
G. S. Patterson, b Cottrell	12	b Rotherham	40
J. B. Thayer. c Turner, b Cottrell	6	b Rotherham	13
W. C. Morgan, not out	45	c Cottrell, b Buckland	1
F. W. Clark, b Cottrell	0	c Bainbridge, b Roller	8
R. S. Newhall, b Cottrell	0	c sub. b Buckland	23
C. A. Newhall, l b w, b Buckland	16	c Fortescue, b Buckland	3
F. W. Ralston, b Roller	11	b Buckland	15
E. T. Comfort, c Rotherham. b Roller	12	not out	0
H. J. Brown, c and b Brown	3	c Cobb, b Buckland	5
W. C. Lowry, b Roller	5	c Turner. b Buckland	2
Extras	9	Extras	11
	128		146

ENGLISH TEAM.

		2nd innings.	
H. W. Bainbridge, l b w, b Brown	8		
W. E. Roller, b Clark	28	c Morgan. b Clark	12
K, J. Kay, c Scott, b Lowry	60	b Clark	2
J. A. Turner, b Clark	0	b Clark	0
E. H. Buckland, c Ralston. b Lowry	82	c and b Brown	7
T. R. Hine-Haycock, b Clark	0	not out	15
A. R. Cobb, b C. A. Newhall	51	not out	3
Rev. A. T. Fortescue, c Morgan, b Lowry	12		
C. E. Cottrell, c C. Newhall, b Lowry	7		
H. Rotherham, not out	5		
F. T. Welman. run out	6		
Extras	6	Extras	1
	265		40

English Team won by six wickets,

Since the above was written, a melancholy occurrence, in the death of Mr. Cobb, has cast quite a gloom over the recollections of the English tour in America. Poor Cobb! Much was he liked by many friends on both sides of the Atlantic, and bitter must have been the sorrow that " surged up " into the hearts of all on hearing of his unexpected death. Cut off by typhoid fever soon after his return home, in the flower of his youth, in the pride of his strength, the memory of his fine manly English character will long be fondly cherished in many an aching and sorrowful heart.